A WORD TO THE WISE
and Other Proverbs

selected by Johanna Hurwitz

illustrated by Robert Rayevsky

Morrow Junior Books
New York

Pen and ink and brilliant watercolors were used for the full-color artwork.
The text type is 18-point ITC Garamond Light.

Text copyright © 1994 by Johanna Hurwitz
Illustrations copyright © 1994 by Robert Rayevsky

Library of Congress Cataloging-in-Publication Data
A word to the wise : and other proverbs / collected by Johanna Hurwitz ; illustrated by
Robert Rayevsky.   p.   cm.   Summary: Presents a list of common proverbs, along with an
explanation of what proverbs are and where they come from.
ISBN 0-688-12065-2.—ISBN 0-688-12066-0 (library)
1. Proverbs—Juvenile literature.   [1. Proverbs.]   I. Hurwitz, Johanna.   II. Rayevsky, Robert, ill.
PN6405.W57   1993   398.9—dc20   93-26836   CIP   AC

These words are for Beni
—J.H.

To Miriam
—R.R.

BENJAMIN FRANKLIN

Preface

Do you know any proverbs? You will probably be surprised to find that you do. Proverbs are short messages of good advice. Some tell us how to act, while others make a general statement from which we can learn something. Proverbs are sometimes called maxims, adages, axioms, or sayings. They are found in every country and every language. Many are anonymous. We don't know who first recited these words of wisdom. They can be found in the Bible. Others are found in books written by great authors throughout history. Horace, Ovid, and Virgil wrote proverbs in Latin. Homer wrote his in Greek, Voltaire and Montaigne wrote theirs in French, and Goethe wrote his in German. Dante wrote proverbs in Italian, and Cervantes in Spanish. Tolstoy wrote his in Russian.

Even if you have never heard of any of these authors, or know their languages, their proverbs have been translated and repeated so often that everyone seems to know their messages. In fact, similar proverbs occur from culture to culture. Every generation has repeated them to the next. This is the way proverbs have been passed on to us.

In the United States, the person most frequently associated with the writing of proverbs is Benjamin Franklin. He lived in the eighteenth century and was a printer, writer, inventor, scientist, and statesman. He signed the Declaration of Independence. But he is also known for having recorded many proverbs in a series of books called *Poor Richard's Almanack*. Benjamin Franklin was aware that there was much for us to learn from the simple truths of proverbs.

The pen is mightier than the sword.

The early bird catches the worm.

A bird in the hand is worth two in the bush.

Out of the frying pan and . . .

into the fire.

A watched pot never boils.

Too many cooks spoil the broth.

A word to the wise is sufficient.

One good turn deserves another.

Misery loves company.

Birds of a feather flock together.

Two heads are better than one.

A poor workman blames his tools.

If a thing is worth doing it is worth doing well.

When the cat's away, the mice will play.

Look before you leap.

Don't count your chickens before they hatch.
Don't cry over spilt milk.

Early to bed, early to rise . . .

makes a man healthy, wealthy, and wise.

All that glitters is not gold.

A fool and his money are soon parted.

Honesty is the best policy.

A good name is better than riches.

He who laughs last laughs best.

Afterword

Proverbs can guide us with their wisdom and they are fun to know and say. However, *there are two sides to every question* (that is a proverb); therefore sometimes proverbs confuse us by contradicting one another. What do you do when two different proverbs give conflicting messages?

Look before you leap.
He who hesitates is lost.

Birds of a feather flock together.
Opposites attract.

Too many cooks spoil the broth.
Many hands make work light.

The early bird catches the worm.
Better late than never.

Haste makes waste. (Also: What we do in haste, we repent at leisure.)
Don't put off till tomorrow what you can do today.

How should one act? In the end, you'll have to make up your own mind because *not to decide is to decide* (that's another proverb). Or perhaps you'll make up a proverb of your own.

The End

A word to the wise.

.9